Published in 2014 by The Rosen Publishing Group, Inc.
29 East 21st Street, New York, NY 10010

## Credits and acknowledgments

**KEY** tl=top left; tc=top center; tr=top right; cl=center left; c=center; cr=center right; bl=bottom left; bc=bottom center; br=bottom right; bg=background

CBT = Corbis; DT = Dreamstime;
GI = Getty Images; iS = istockphoto.com; PDCD = PhotoDisc;
SH = Shutterstock; wiki = Wikipedia

**front cover** CBT; **2–3**tc SH; **4–5**cl SH; **6–7**bc iS; **7**cr, tl iS; **8**bl iS; br, cr, tr PDCD; **9**c, cl, tc, tr iS; bl, cr, tl PDCD; cr, tl SH; **10**cl DT; bc SH; **10–11**c SH; **11**br CBT; tr SH; **12**bc iS; **12–13**bl N; **13**tl DT; br, cl, cr, tr iS; tc SH; **14**br wiki; **15**bl GI; **16**bl, tl DT; cl iS; **17**br CBT; tr N; **18**tr iS; tl SH; **18–19**tc SH; **19**c, cr iS; **20**bc DT; bg iS; tl SH; **21**bg, tr iS; **24**tl DT; bc, cl iS; **24–25**tr SH; **25**br SH; **28**bg, bl, br, cl iS; cr wiki; **29**bc, bg, tl, tr iS; br wiki

All illustrations copyright Weldon Owen Pty Ltd

Weldon Owen Pty Ltd
Managing Director:  Kay Scarlett
Creative Director:  Sue Burk
Publisher:  Helen Bateman
Senior Vice President, International Sales:  Stuart Laurence
Vice President Sales North America:  Ellen Towell
Administration Manager, International Sales:  Kristine Ravn

Library of Congress Cataloging-in-Publication Data

Coupe, Robert, author.
  Force and motion / by Robert Coupe.
      pages cm. — (Discovery education—how it works)
  Includes index.
  ISBN 978-1-4777-6317-9 (library) — ISBN 978-1-4777-6318-6 (pbk.) —
ISBN 978-1-4777-6319-3 (6-pack)
  1.  Force and energy—Juvenile literature. 2.  Motion—Juvenile literature. 3.  Simple machines—Juvenile literature.  I. Title.
  QC73.4.C68 2014
  531.6—dc23
                              2013023585

Manufactured in the United States of America

CPSIA Compliance Information: Batch #W14PK2: For Further Information contact Rosen Publishing, New York, New York at 1-800-237-9932

# HOW IT WORKS

# FORCE AND MOTION

ROBERT COUPE

**PowerKiDS**
press.

New York

# Contents

# What Are Forces?

Forces are pushes and pulls that make things move and stop moving. They also control how quickly or how slowly things move. You may not be aware of it, but forces are acting on you all the time, even when you are sitting still or when you are asleep. Just to breathe, you need to force air in and out of your body.

Forces that you may not notice also act upon you. Gravity, for example, is a force that keeps you on the ground and stops you from floating up into the air.

**Scoring a point**
Basketball players use pushing forces to hurl the ball upward toward the basket. The players push the basketball upward over the hoop, then the force of gravity makes it fall back down to the ground.

**Pulling a rubber band**
When you hold a stretched rubber band, you use forces in your hand, thumb, and finger muscles. These forces act against the forces in the rubber band, which are trying to pull the rubber band back to its smaller size.

## Pulling a trailer

When you move, you use energy in your body to produce the force to make your muscles work. A car pulling a trailer gets its energy from the fuel in its engine. This energy creates the force that makes the car and trailer move.

## Arm wrestling

When you pick up a piece of paper, you use forces in your arm and hand muscles. To pick up a heavy book, you need more force. When two strong people arm wrestle, they use as much force as their arms and hands can produce.

## Playing squash

Squash is a very fast game. When a squash racket hits a squash ball, the force of the contact causes the ball to fly quickly toward the wall. When it strikes the wall, the force of that contact sends it speeding back into the court.

# Simple Machines

Machines help to make work easier. Some of the machines in use today, such as washing machines and airplanes, are very complex and are made up of many moving parts.

In ancient times, people used simple machines to help them carry out basic tasks. They used ramps to move things to a higher level. They used pulleys or levers to lift up things. They used wheels and axles in carts and chariots. Complex machines use different combinations of the six basic types of simple machines: inclined planes, wedges, screws, pulleys, wheels and axles, and levers.

## 1 Inclined plane

An inclined plane, or ramp, makes it easier to pull or push things upward. It reduces the force required. When ancient Egyptians built pyramids, they used inclined planes to move blocks of stone upward.

## 2 Wedge

A wedge is a sharp edge or point that forces its way into something, such as a block of wood. Nails and axes are examples of wedge machines.

## 3 Screw

A screw can have a sharp, pointed end and grooves that go upward in a spiral. Force applied to the top of the spiral causes the screw to bore downward into wood or other materials.

## HOW LEVERS WORK

A lever is a long rod or stick that rests on a point called a fulcrum. When you apply force to one end of a lever, it reduces the effort needed to lift or move a load. People in ancient Egypt used levers, called shadoofs, to lift bucketfuls of water from the Nile River.

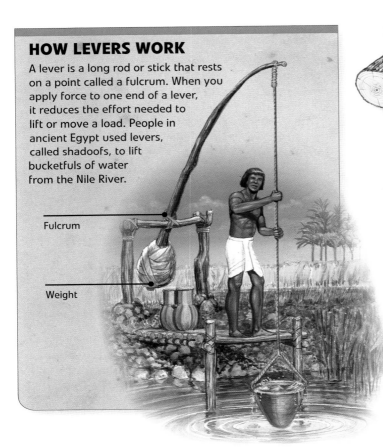

Fulcrum

Weight

**4**

## Pulley

Raising a sail on a boat, or a flag on a flagpole, requires a pulley. This is a rope or wire that goes over one or more wheels. The rope is pulled at one end to raise up a load.

**6** **Types of levers**

### Wheelbarrow

The load of a wheelbarrow is quite close to its fulcrum at the wheel. When you lift the wheelbarrow's handles, you can lift and move heavy loads.

### Rowing boat oar

The load at the end of an oar is the force from the water you need to row through to make the boat move. The fulcrum is where the oar pivots on the boat.

**5**

## Wheel and axle

A car or a bike has wheels and axles that hold the wheels in place. An axle is a rod in the center of a wheel. It attaches the wheel to another part of a machine or to other wheels.

### Crowbar

This long metal rod has a curved end as its fulcrum. By applying force at the end of the crowbar, it is possible to overcome much bigger forces and pry apart materials that have been secured together.

### Nutcracker

The fulcrum on a nutcracker is the point where the two handles are joined together. The nut that is to be cracked open is the load. Force is applied with your hands on the ends of the handle.

# Complex Machines

A machine is said to be complex if it uses two or more simple machines. Many machines do their job by changing the size or direction of a force. Before it can start working, a machine needs a source of energy. In many machines, human muscle power provides this energy. Throughout the ages, animals have been used to power many complex machines, such as chariots and plows.

Gears are also important parts of many machines. Gears consist of two or more wheels with teeth or cogs that fit into each other.

**Eggbeater**
An eggbeater has two gear wheels: a big wheel at the top and a much smaller one underneath, just above the blades. When the handle is turned at a certain speed, the gears cause the blades to turn at a much greater speed.

**Can opener**
A can opener works when force is applied to the handles, which are levers. This forces the sharp cutting wheel down until it pierces the top of the can. When the cutting wheel handle is turned, the gear turns and makes the can rotate.

### Reeling in fish

The spool that holds a fishing line, which spins around as the line goes out, is wound in by a gear and pulley. It allows the line length to be locked and then wound in, preventing the fish from pulling the line back out.

Pulley

Wheel
and axle

### Riding a bicycle

The cogs on a bicycle's gear wheels fit into a chain. When the pedals are pushed, the chain transfers the movement to the wheels. A force called friction helps the tires grip the road surface and slows the bicycle down when the brakes are applied.

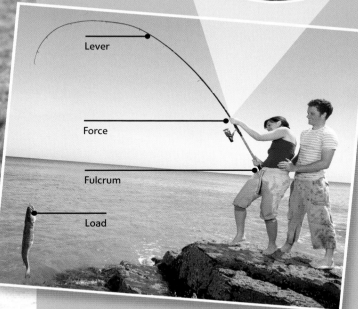

Lever

Force

Fulcrum

Load

### Fishing rod

This lever is made of strong material that can bend without breaking. The fulcrum on this lever is where the end of the rod is held, perhaps at the fisherman's hip. The lever requires a large force, but a small movement can pull a large fish clear of the water.

# Forces and Energy

Forces make things move, go faster, move in a different direction, or slow down and stop. Behind every force is a source of energy that makes it work.

In very complex machines, energy can come from fuels such as coal, gasoline, rocket fuel, or electric power. In fast-moving machines, such as jet aircraft, race cars, and spacecraft, huge amounts of energy are needed to start this movement and keep it up against opposing friction forces. In many sports, people train their bodies so their muscles can transfer as much energy as possible to objects they throw or strike.

## Space shuttle

Space shuttles carry astronauts out of Earth's atmosphere and into space. Rocket fuel provides the energy needed to propel these machines skyward. When rocket fuel burns, it produces hot gases. These gases push it upward with tremendous force as they rush outward through a nozzle beneath the shuttle.

## Electric vacuum cleaner

The energy for a modern vacuum cleaner comes from electricity. An electric motor drives a spinning fan that sucks up air, dust, and dirt from the floor through a hose. The dust goes into a bag and air escapes through tiny holes in the bag.

## Lawn mower

A fuel lawn mower is driven by gasoline, and the mower's engine does most of the work. The person behind the mower has only to push it along. In earlier times, people used scythes to cut grass. This was exhausting work that needed a huge amount of human energy.

## Javelin throwing

Arms and legs are types of levers, and muscles apply large forces on them. Champion javelin throwers have developed very strong muscles. They use fast movement and huge strength to apply great force from their arms to the javelin they are hurling forward.

## *That's Amazing!*

As it goes into orbit, a space shuttle reaches a traveling speed of more than 17,000 miles (27,400 km) per hour.

## Horse and carriage

Before the motor car was invented, and still in many places today, horses and other animals provided the energy needed for people to move around in carriages and carts. On farms, strong oxen pulled heavy plows that tilled the land.

# Machines at Work

Machines convert energy from fuel into movement. In the 1800s and early 1900s, steam powered most machines, factories, and vehicles, such as ships, trains, and early cars. Water that was boiled over burning coal or wood produced the steam. The force of the steam, released under pressure, drove pistons that then applied the force to wheels, gears, levers, and pulleys.

Today's internal combustion engines, such as those in cars, convert energy much more quickly. But even now, most of our electric power is produced by big, steam-driven machines called turbines.

**Boiler**
Water was fed into the boiler and steam was forced out under pressure through narrow pipes.

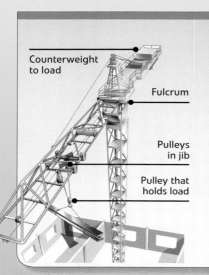

Counterweight to load

Fulcrum

Pulleys in jib

Pulley that holds load

## HOW A TOWER CRANE WORKS

A tower crane consists of a long lever, called a jib, that is mounted on a high steel tower. The top of the tower is the fulcrum, between a load on one end and a counterweight on the other. Pulleys along the jib transfer force to a pulley underneath that lifts and lowers the load.

**Engine time line**
The first steam engine was invented almost 2,000 years ago. It showed that steam under pressure could create fast movement. It was not until much later, however, that the first useful steam engine was developed.

**AD 60**
The Greek engineer Hero invented a steam engine more than 2,000 years ago. He boiled water in a sphere until steam from the nozzle made the sphere turn around at high speed.

**1712**
In England, Thomas Newcomen invented a steam engine that could pump water out of mines. James Watt developed this design to create more complex steam engines.

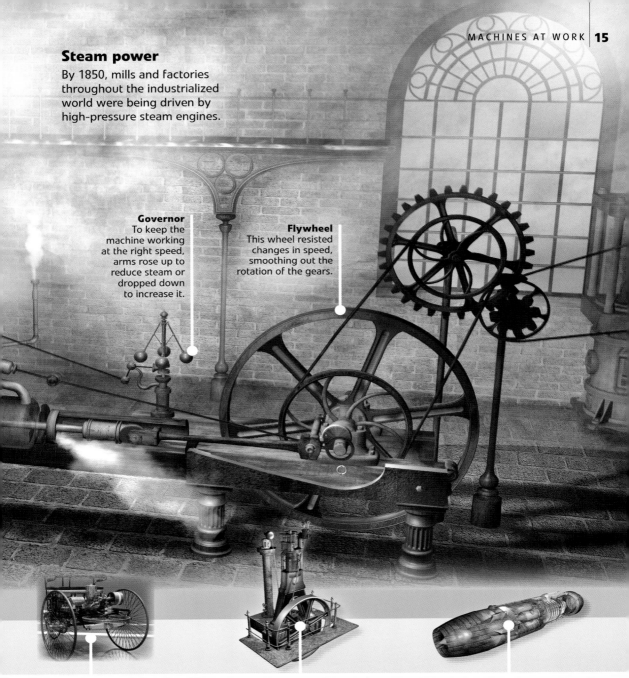

## Steam power

By 1850, mills and factories throughout the industrialized world were being driven by high-pressure steam engines.

**Governor**
To keep the machine working at the right speed, arms rose up to reduce steam or dropped down to increase it.

**Flywheel**
This wheel resisted changes in speed, smoothing out the rotation of the gears.

**1859**
Belgian inventor Étienne Lenoir converted a steam engine so that it could run on coal gas inside the piston. German Nikolaus Otto later improved on this design.

**1892**
German Rudolph Diesel designed a more complex and powerful type of combustion engine that was suited to running heavy vehicles, tractors, and boats.

**1937**
Frank Whittle built the first working jet engine. Jet engines force air into a tube where it is compressed, mixed with fuel for combustion, then shot out the other end to produce thrust.

**Egg timer**
With an egg timer, gravity causes grains of sand to trickle downward through a narrow opening, from the top of the container to the part underneath. The time it takes for all the sand to fall through to the lower chamber is the time it takes to boil an egg.

**Pouring**
Gravity can be seen at work in all kinds of everyday activities. When you drink from a glass, cup, or a bottle, you have to hold the container higher than your mouth. When you pour mixture into a baking dish, it is Earth's gravity that pulls it down.

**Showerhead**
During a shower, water pours down from the showerhead. Pressure forces water through the pipes, but without the force of gravity, the water would not drip off you and go down the drain.

# Gravity

Gravity is a pulling force that causes objects to move toward each other. Planet Earth has a strong gravitational pull that attracts objects toward its center. That is why we stay on the ground and do not float in the air, and why things we drop fall to the ground.

The Sun's strong gravity keeps the planets orbiting around it. Earth's gravity holds the Moon in its orbit around Earth. The Moon and the Sun pull on Earth's oceans to create tides.

# AIR RESISTANCE AND GRAVITY

Gravity pulls everything downward. But there is another force, known as air resistance, that works against falling objects. Pushing upward, air resistance makes very light objects, or objects with a wide surface area, fall more slowly than heavier objects.

### Same size
If you drop a tennis ball and an apple from the same height, even though the apple is heavier, it will hit the ground at almost the same time as the tennis ball.

### Different sizes
If you drop a sheet of paper and a pencil, the paper will float down much more slowly because of upward air resistance over the much larger area of paper.

### Floating free
Astronauts in space are farther from the center of Earth than when they are on the ground, so the force of gravity is less. In space, astronauts "fall" around Earth and feel weightless, although they are not.

### No air resistance
In a place where there is no air, such as the surface of the Moon, an apple and a very light feather would hit the surface at exactly the same time if they were dropped from exactly the same height.

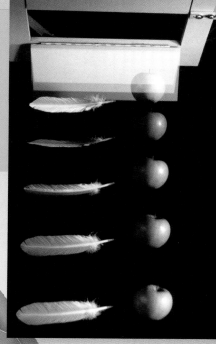

### Roller coaster ride
If you ski down a steep, snowy slope, gravity pulls you downward. In a roller coaster ride, a motor pulls a train of cars attached to rails to the top of a slope. Gravity then causes the train to plunge downward at an ever-increasing speed.

### 1 Jumping

This bungee jumper throws himself off a platform high above a deep canyon. His ankles are clamped together and are attached firmly to a long and very strong elastic cord. The cord is also attached to a body harness.

### 2 Falling

As this bungee jumper falls downward, there is very little air resistance. His body falls faster and faster because gravity causes falling objects to accelerate.

# Defying Gravity

A ir resistance is one of the forces that reduce the effect of gravity. Upward air resistance, spread over a wide area, allows parachute jumpers to fall slowly to the ground, instead of crashing into it. It helps gliders to stay aloft and kites to stay flying. The force of a huge upward push, or thrust, sends space shuttles soaring upward, and the powerful thrust produced by jet engines, combined with lift forces from the wings, keeps aircraft flying forward.

### Thrill seekers

Some people jump out of airplanes for fun. At first they hurtle downward, but when they open their parachute, they slow their fall. Bungee jumpers jump off platforms, bridges, and other high places for the thrill of experiencing the downward force of gravity.

> Some bungee jumpers start on the ground. A stretched elastic cord is released, pulling them upward. Gravity then pulls them downward.

**3 Reaching the end**
When this jumper has come to the end of the cord, his fall begins to slow. He plunges a little farther down as the elastic fibers in the cord expand to their full extent.

**4 Springing back**
The elastic fibers in the cord retract and pull a bungee jumper's body upward again. When they are fully retracted, these fibers expand again as gravity pulls the body downward.

**5 Coming to rest**
An upside-down bungee jumper bounces up and down until, finally, gravity and the force from the cord are balanced. This bungee jumper hangs still at the end of the cord until she is winched back up to the platform.

**Striking matches**
A modern safety match is ignited
by pulling the match head
strongly against the rough side
of the matchbox. The friction this
creates produces enough heat
to cause the phosphorus in the
match head to burst into flame.

# Friction

When two surfaces touch and rub together, they create a force called friction. Friction acts to slow movement down.

The amount of friction created depends on how smooth or rough the surfaces are. If you roll a tennis ball across a grass lawn, it will slow down more quickly than if you roll it with the same force along a smooth pathway. The friction between a car's tires and a dry road is much stronger than the friction between the same tires and an icy road.

**Smoking tires**
Friction produces heat. The stronger the friction, the more heat it will produce. If a car brakes or skids suddenly on a road surface, the amount of heat this creates can cause smoke to appear from beneath the wheels as rubber from the tires burns.

### Skateboarding

Skateboarders use friction to control the speed at which they travel. The friction between the wheels and the surface helps to limit the speed. When a skateboard changes direction suddenly, the increase in friction slows it down or stops it completely.

### *Did You Know?*

Fire can be made from the friction caused by rubbing sticks of wood together with great force.

## Sorting metals

Magnets have many uses in industry. They are used, for example, in all electric motors and generators. Huge, powerful magnets can be used to separate magnetic metals, such as iron, steel, and nickel, from nonmagnetic metals, such as aluminum.

**Magnetic poles**

Like Earth, a magnet has poles—a north pole at one end and a south pole at the other. A magnetic field joins them. If you bring similar poles of two magnets near each other, the magnets will try to push apart. If you bring opposite poles near each other, they try to pull together.

# Magnetism and Static Electricity

S ome forces act without the need for objects to touch each other. Magnetism and the electrostatic force are invisible forces that work from a distance.

Iron and some other metals can act as magnets that pull other metals toward them or push them farther away. The area around a magnet in which it is able to push or pull other metals is called a magnetic field. There is a strong magnetic field inside Earth, which reaches far out into space. When an electric current runs through a wire, it produces a magnetic field around the wire.

**Pointing north**
Over the centuries, compasses have helped countless travelers to find their way. A compass's needle always points north. It is attracted to one of the poles of Earth's magnetic field, which is near the geographic North Pole.

## STATIC ELECTRICITY

Sometimes when things rub together, the contact causes a separation of electrical charge. This is called static electricity. Cut up some tissue paper into small pieces. Blow up a balloon and rub it fast a few times against a woolen sweater. Bring the balloon close to the paper and see what happens.

**1 Charging up**
Rubbing a balloon against a sweater's rough surface separates charges.

**2 Pulling power**
The static electricity attracts the paper to the balloon.

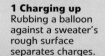

North pole

South pole

Magnetic field lines

**Attracting**
The north and south poles of two magnets attract each other.

**Repelling**
The south poles of these magnets repel each other.

### Ancient dome
The Pantheon, in Rome, Italy, was built almost 2,000 years ago. Its domed ceiling is made of concrete, covered with brick. Heavy walls support the dome, and less dense materials are used in the walls and dome as they get higher. This reduces the weight and helps to explain why it does not fall down.

### Flying buttresses
Many old Gothic churches in Europe have high, thin, stone walls, with large areas of glass windows. These walls would fall outward were it not for flying buttresses. These support the walls by transferring the outward force downward to the ground.

Keystone

Force

Force

### Archway
The force of gravity pulls down on the weight of the material above an arch. The central stone, or keystone, in the center and at the top of the arch redirects this force sideways and stops the arch from falling down.

# Structures

Buildings of all kinds—houses, skyscrapers, bridges, dams—have forces that work on them. If a building is to remain standing and not fall down or become damaged, it must be able to stand up to these forces. Some of these forces are structural. When some parts of a building put stress on other parts, the forces that act against each other need to be balanced. Gravity is a force that acts on all buildings. Outside forces, such as wind, earthquakes, and how people use the buildings, also put stress on them.

**Suspension bridge**
The Golden Gate Bridge in San Francisco is a suspension bridge. Strong steel cables stretch between two towers, and other steel cables that hang from them hold up the deck, or road, of the bridge. Cables also attach the towers to the ground to prevent them from falling inward.

**Arched bridge**
In a steel, arched bridge, cables or tie-bars hanging from a wide arch hold up the deck, or road. Forces push outward to each end of the arch and are then transferred to the ground. The Sydney Harbour Bridge, in Sydney, Australia, is a famous example.

# Why Ships Do Not Sink

A ship will float so long as the weight of the ship, plus the air it contains, is less than the weight of the displaced water.

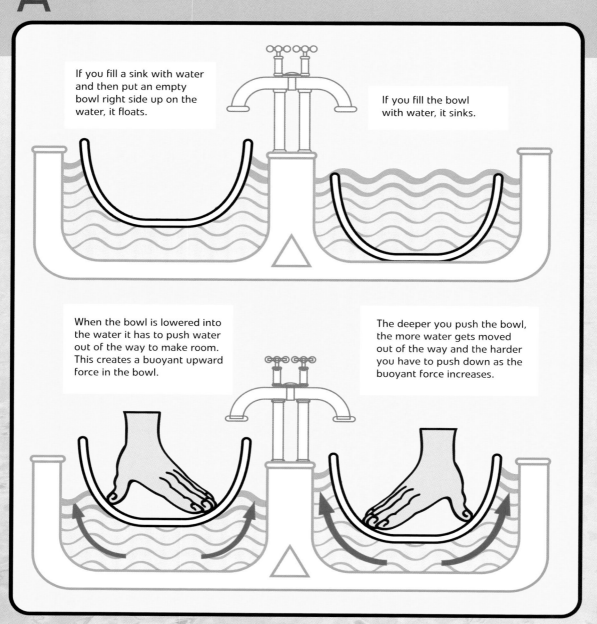

If you fill a sink with water and then put an empty bowl right side up on the water, it floats.

If you fill the bowl with water, it sinks.

When the bowl is lowered into the water it has to push water out of the way to make room. This creates a buoyant upward force in the bowl.

The deeper you push the bowl, the more water gets moved out of the way and the harder you have to push down as the buoyant force increases.

### EUREKA!

According to one legend, the ancient Greek inventor Archimedes yelled "Eureka!" when he got into a bath and noticed that the water level rose. He suddenly understood that the volume of water displaced must be the same as the volume of his body. "Eureka" means "I have found it!"

Archimedes made an important discovery while having a bath.

**AIR**

### All afloat

If a boat is mostly air inside, the hull can be very heavy, but the total weight of the hull, plus air, can still be much less than the weight of the displaced water, and so the boat will float. If a boat gets a hole in the hull, however, it fills with water. This displaces the air, making the boat heavier than the water it is displacing. So the boat sinks.

# Discovering Forces

Over the centuries, scientists and philosophers have been devising theories and conducting experiments to explain how forces work and why objects move in certain ways. The ancient Greek philosopher Aristotle had many ideas about motion and gravity. It was almost another 2,000 years before scientists, such as Sir Isaac Newton and Galileo Galilei, were able to show that many of Aristotle's ideas were mistaken.

Later scientists, such as Albert Einstein, used Newton's and Galileo's findings to make more discoveries. Science works by building on earlier discoveries and mistakes.

### Fact or Fiction?

Galileo is said to have demonstrated his ideas about gravity by dropping cannonballs and much lighter balls from high up on the leaning tower in Pisa, Italy. This is most likely fiction.

**Aristotle** (384–322 BC)
This ancient Athenian wrote many books. One is called *Physics,* and in it he explained how he thought gravity worked. He thought objects and substances moved up or down according to where they naturally belonged. Steam and gases moved upward toward the heavens. Solid objects moved downward to Earth.

**Archimedes** (287–212 BC)
As well as discovering the principle of the displacement of water, which led to our understanding of why objects can float, Archimedes used mathematics to show how levers worked. He also constructed systems of pulleys to make lifting easier.

### Galileo Galilei (1564–1642)

The Italian Galileo Galilei conducted experiments and made important discoveries about gravity. He explained that objects of different weights, when dropped from the same height, fall and gather speed at the exact same rate. He also investigated how friction acted on moving objects.

### Sir Isaac Newton (1643–1727)

English scientist Sir Isaac Newton published his famous *Principia*, showing that gravity explained the notion of the planets and that every particle of matter exerted a pull of gravity on every other particle. He also greatly improved our understanding of how and why things move.

### Albert Einstein (1879–1955)

Perhaps the greatest scientist of the twentieth century, Albert Einstein published his paper on the general theory of relativity in 1915.
This explained, among other things, that gravity could be regarded as a "bending" of space by matter. This influenced the paths that planets followed in their orbit around the Sun.

# Glossary

**accelerate**
(ik-SEH-luh-rayt)
To increase the speed at
which an object or a body
is traveling.

**air resistance**
(ER rih-ZIS-tens)
The force that opposes the
motion of an object
through air.

**astronauts** (AS-truh-nots)
People who travel and work
in space, outside
Earth's atmosphere.

**Athenian**
(uh-THEE-nee-un)
A person who is a citizen
of the city of Athens,
in Greece.

**axle** (AK-sul)
A rod running through
the center of a wheel.
The wheel turns around
its axle.

**compass** (KUM-pus)
An instrument that people
use to find direction.

**electric charge**
(ih-LEK-trik CHARJ)
A property of matter that
results in electric forces
between particles.

**energy** (EH-nur-jee)
The quantity that allows
objects and other things to
move, heat up, or do other
kinds of work.

**friction** (FRIK-shin)
The force between two
objects or substances when
they rub together.

**fuel** (FYOOL)
A substance, such as wood,
coal, gasoline, or diesel, that
can be burned to provide
heat or produce the energy
to drive an engine.

**fulcrum** (FUL-krum)
Something that supports a
lever, and the point about
which the lever pivots.

**gasoline** (ga-suh-LEEN)
A liquid made from oil that
burns easily and is used as a
fuel for motor vehicles,
aircraft, and other machines.

**glider** (GLY-der)
An aircraft that has no
engine and flies by riding on
air currents.

**Gothic** (GAH-thik)
A style of architecture that
was used in Europe between
the 1100s and the 1500s.

**gravity** (GRA-vih-tee)
The force that pulls objects
down to the ground and
keeps Earth and other
planets moving in orbit
around the Sun.

**internal combustion
engine**
(in-TUR-nul kum-BUS-chun
EN-jun)
An engine, such as one inside
a car or jet plane, inside
which fuel is burned.

**lever** (LEH-vur)
A rod or bar that pivots at
one point, the fulcrum, in
response to a force and a
load applied elsewhere on
the bar.

**magnetism**
(MAG-nuh-tih-zum)
An effect that exerts forces
on certain (magnetic)
materials and on
electric currents.

**muscles** (MUH-sulz)
Tissues within the bodies
of humans and animals that
are attached to bones
and organs.

**phosphorus** (FOS-fur-us)
A highly reactive element
used in matches, which
bursts into flame if heat or
friction is applied to it.

**pulley** (PUL-lee)
A wheel with a groove around its rim that is used to change the direction of a force .

**ramp** (RAMP)
A flat surface that rises on a slope from one level to a higher level.

**scythe** (SYTH)
A tool with a long wooden handle and a long, sharp, curved blade that was used in earlier times to cut grasses and crops, such as wheat.

**shadoof** (shuh-DOOF)
A type of lever with a bucket on one end.

**space shuttle**
(SPAYS SHUH-tul)
A reusable spacecraft that takes astronauts into space and back to Earth.

**static electricity**
(STA-tik ih-lek-TRIH-suh-tee)
An electric charge that does not flow in a current, but can be produced by contact between certain kinds of surfaces when they are rubbed together.

**steam engine**
(STEEM EN-jun)
An engine that uses steam under pressure to produce the motion needed to make the engine work.

**turbine** (TUR-byn)
A wheel with blades that a gas, such as steam, or a liquid, such as water, forces to turn at great speed.

**wedge** (WEJ)
An object with a sharp edge that can be forced between two objects to push them apart or hold them in place.

# Index

## A
air resistance 17, 18
Archimedes 27, 28
Aristotle 28
axle 8, 9, 11

## B
bridges 18, 25
buildings 24, 25

## D
Diesel, Rudolph 15

## E
Egyptians 8
Einstein, Albert 28, 29
elastic 18, 19
electricity 12, 23
energy 7, 10, 12, 13, 14

## F
friction 11, 12, 20, 21, 23, 29
fuel 7, 12, 13, 14

## G
Galileo Galilei 28, 29

gears 10, 11, 14
gravity 6, 16, 17, 18, 19, 24, 25, 28, 29

## H
heat 20
Hero 14

## I
internal combustion engine 14, 15

## J
jet engines 15, 18

## L
Lenoir, Étienne 15
levers 8, 10, 11, 13, 14, 28

## M
magnetism 22, 23
muscles 6, 7, 10, 12, 13

## N
Newcomen, Thomas 14
Newton, Sir Isaac 28, 29

## P
pulleys 8, 9, 11, 14, 28

## R
ramps 8
relativity, general theory of 29
rubber band 6

## S
screw 8
shadoof 8
ships 26, 27
skateboarding 21
space shuttle 12, 13
sports, forces in 6, 7, 13, 18, 19
static electricity 23
steam 14, 15, 28

## W
water displacement 26, 27, 28
Watt, James 14
wheels 8, 9, 10, 11, 14
Whittle, Frank 15

# Websites

Due to the changing nature of Internet links, PowerKids Press has developed an online list of websites related to the subject of this book. This site is updated regularly. Please use this link to access the list:
www.powerkidslinks.com/disc/force/